THE GEEK'S
COOKBOOK

Easy Recipes Inspired by Pokémon, Harry Potter, Star Wars, and More!

By **Liguori Lecomte**
Translated by **Andrea Jones Berasaluce**
Photography by **Pierre Chivoret**
Design by **Alexia Janny**

Skyhorse Publishing

ACKNOWLEDGMENTS

Writing this book required a little madness, a few all-nighters, but also some collaboration.
Thanks to Éditions Solar for their trust and support in this adventure.
Thanks to the students in my geek workshops.
Thanks to Cam and Clem for that promo photo.
Finally, thank you to those around me here and those watching me from above.

Skyhorse Publishing books may be purchased in bulk at special discounts for sales promotion, corporate gifts, fund-raising, or educational purposes. Special editions can also be created to specifications. For details, contact the Special Sales Department, Skyhorse Publishing, 307 West 36th Street, 11th Floor, New York, NY 10018 or info@skyhorsepublishing.com.

Skyhorse® and Skyhorse Publishing® are registered trademarks of Skyhorse Publishing, Inc.®, a Delaware corporation.

Visit our website at www.skyhorsepublishing.com.

10 9 8 7 6 5 4 3 2

Library of Congress Cataloging-in-Publication Data is available on file.

Cover design by Michael Short
Editorial director: Didier Férat
Copyediting: Diane Monserat
Graphics & Design: Julia Philipps
Production: Laurence Duboscq

ISBN: 978-1-5107-2923-0
eISBN: 978-1-5107-2927-8

Printed in China

Intro

When people ask chefs where their passion for cooking comes from, the typical response is always to declare the love that they've had for pots and pans since childhood, or to talk about their cherished grandma's recipes that they've had since they were fifteen years old.

Personally, at that age I was more likely to be watching the extended editions of *The Lord of the Rings* trilogy, or spending hours on my gaming console.

I am often asked what kind of chef I am . . . and I always answer that I see myself as a kind of "food gamer."

And that has never been truer than it is today with the release of *The Geek's Cookbook.*

I hope you will enjoy lots of great times with your friends thanks to the recipes inspired by pop culture in this book.

The aim of this small culinary journey is to show that cooking can be geeky, and geeky can be chic, delicious, and easy, even for noobs.

—Liguori Lecomte

Who am I?

Liguori Lecomte is a hip, young twenty-eight-year-old chef and a true "food gamer" interested in all types of cuisine. Brought up on pop culture, he brings a touch of geek to his recipes. He has been running his fun and offbeat cooking workshops since the end of 2013. These days, you can of course find him on the internet, where he continues to share his chef's secrets.

Geek Universes: A User Guide

🐉 Harry Potter

This literary œuvre by J. K. Rowling comprises seven books published between 1997 and 2007, detailing the adventures of young wizard Harry Potter and his friends. A genuine best seller, with 450 million copies sold worldwide, fans have been rewarded with eight blockbuster films, too.

🐉 The Matrix

We were able to enter the Matrix with Neo thanks to Lana and Lilly Wachowski and their film trilogy released between 1999 and 2003 (Warner Bros. production). On the strength of its numerous awards in the 2000s, *The Matrix* is one of the biggest science fiction films of its generation.

🐉 The Lord of the Rings

The *Lord of the Rings* trilogy was written by J. R. R. Tolkien and published in 1954 and 1955. With its portrayal of creative characters and creatures, the invention of languages, the composing of songs . . . it is a monumental work! Director Peter Jackson brought the saga of Frodo and his One Ring to the big screen masterfully between 2001 and 2003.

🐉 Star Wars

George Lucas's saga spans generations. After the six films released between 1977 and 2005, *Star Wars: The Force Awakens* kicked off a new trilogy of saga films in 2015. The battles between the Jedi Knights and the Sith have been so successful that the franchise has also appeared in novels, cartoons, video games, and TV series, creating a whole new empire!

📺 Breaking Bad

One of the very best series from the United States, which acquired a worldwide fan base, Vince Gilligan's creation is a must for TV fans. With a total of sixty-two episodes spread over five seasons between 2008 and 2013, its success is also due to the talents of its two leading actors, Bryan Cranston and Aaron Paul.

📺 Dexter

Created by James Manos Jr. from the novels by Jeff Lindsay, Dexter covered eight seasons, with a total of ninety-six episodes screened between 2006 and 2013. The cult aspect of the series lies in the fact that you soon become drawn to the shy and kind Dexter Morgan, who also happens to be a serial killer!

📺 Game of Thrones

Adapted from the novels written by George R. R. Martin, the first of which was published in 1996, *Game of Thrones* is the stand-out TV series in the medieval-fantasy genre. Brought to the screen by David Benioff and D. B. Weiss, it numbers sixty episodes to date over six seasons (since 2011) and has become the most widely shown series in the world.

📺 The Big Bang Theory

This US sitcom is the brainchild of a collaboration between Chuck Lorre and Bill Prady. Littered with pop-culture references, the series numbers 207 episodes to date over nine seasons and highlights the contrast beween the intelligence of a group of geeks and the social skills of their new neighbor.

⏻ Minecraft

Minecraft is a game developed by the Swedish game designer Markus Persson and published by Mojang. Immersed in an unpredictable voxel-based universe, the player uses its natural resources to progress. The game has sold more than one hundred million copies in seven years.

⏻ The Legend of Zelda

Comprising eighteen games and a host of spinoffs, *The Legend of Zelda* adventure series, in which the hero Link has to save Princess Zelda, was created by Shigeru Miyamoto and Takashi Tezuka for Nintendo. Apart from record sales for some of the games, *Zelda* is particularly known for the extent of its worlds, its gameplay, its Second Quests, and its music.

⏻ Final Fantasy

With a global reputation in the video game world, *Final Fantasy* is the creation of Hironobu Sakaguchi and produced by Square Enix. Available on numerous consoles, this role-playing game, with different stories in each episode, brings together the best of the video-game arts (gameplay, graphics, design, music), earning it multiple film adaptations on the big screen!

💬 The Walking Dead

A comic book series, *The Walking Dead* was written by Robert Kirkman and illustrated by Tony Moore. The pitch: After a global epidemic, a handful of survivors have to contend with the rest of the population, who have turned into zombies. The first issue was published by Image Comics in 2003. Kirkman subsequently approached television producers with his idea, and the first TV episode was adapted and screened in 2010. Kirkman's universe has also transferred to novels and video games.

💬 Pokémon

Television series, films, cards, manga . . . pokémania is thanks to the international success of the Nintendo game developed by Satoshi Tajiri in 1996, which has smashed numerous records. The Pokémon Company and Niantic's smartphone app Pokémon Go brought capturing pokémon back on trend in 2016.

💬 Batman

Created by Bob Kane in 1939, the legendary righter of wrongs has matured a great deal over time—although without a single wrinkle. The character has since been adapted for television, cartoons, and feature films, as well as video games.

. . . STARTING OUT

Glazing Vegetables

SERVES 2

Preparation time: 10 mins

Cooking time: 5–10 mins

7 oz Vegetables (carrots, turnips, pearl onions, etc.)

¾ oz Butter

1 T Superfine sugar

3½ fl oz Water

Salt and pepper

Wash and peel the vegetables (*Image 1*).

Make balls from the vegetables using a melon baller (or cubes, or rounds, or something else) (*Image 2*).

Place the vegetables, butter, sugar, and water in a saucepan (the water should reach no more than halfway up the sides of the vegetables), season to taste with salt and pepper, and bring to a boil (*Image 3*).

Cook over medium heat for 5–10 minutes, depending on the size of the vegetables. When the water has evaporated, the butter-sugar mixture coats the vegetables and makes them glossy (*Image 4*).

1

Notes

It's better to start with less water and add more if needed to finish cooking the vegetables than to start with too much and have to throw out the tasty liquid!

Smoking Food with Hay

Foods to be smoked
(chicken, fish,
potatoes, butter . . .)

Hay

Aromatic herbs
(thyme, bay leaf . . .)

1 Large, heavy saucepan

1 Wire rack

Blowtorch

1 Lid or cover

Plastic wrap

First, cook the food to be smoked (for example, frying, sautéeing, broiling).

Secondly, make an express smoker: place a little hay in the bottom of the saucepan with your choice of aromatic herbs. Place the wire rack on top of the hay, so that the food to be smoked isn't in contact with the hay (*Image 1*).

Next, place the cooked food on the rack (*Image 2*). Carefully light the hay with a blowtorch, without scorching the food (*Image 3*).

Once the fire has taken hold, cover the saucepan with a lid and seal with plastic wrap to extinguish the flames and trap the smoke (*Image 4*). Wait 5–10 minutes before removing the lid and taking out the smoked food.

Notes

Smoking doesn't cook the food. It gives cooked foods a smoky flavor without charring its surface.

...CINEMA

HARRY POTTER

Poached Ravenclaw with Forbidden Forest Vegetables

SERVES 4

Preparation time: 45 mins

Cooking time: 45 mins

1 T Chicken bouillon powder

4 Chicken breast fillets

For the bacon sauce:

3 ½ oz Thick-cut bacon

10 fl oz Whipping cream

For the vegetables:

5 ½ oz Chanterelle mushrooms

5 ½ oz White mushrooms

3 ½ oz Black trumpet mushrooms

3 ½ oz Oyster mushrooms

3 ¼ oz Butter

2 Parsnips

1 T Superfine sugar

12 Fingerling potatoes

1 pinch Coarse salt

Salt and pepper

In a saucepan, dissolve the chicken bouillon powder in 2 pints (4 cups) of water. Add the chicken and cook over medium heat for 15–20 minutes, depending on the size of the fillets. Make sure the liquid doesn't boil but stays just at simmering point. Take out the chicken, then bring the broth to a boil and reduce it by about three-quarters to make 1 cup to use in the bacon sauce.

Make the bacon sauce: Cut the bacon into lardons. Pour the cream into a saucepan and add the bacon. Bring to a boil, then remove from the heat, cover, and infuse for 10 minutes. Add the cup of reduced chicken broth and reheat the mixture. Strain with a fine metal strainer to remove the solids. Adjust the seasoning if necessary.

Prepare the vegetables: Trim the mushrooms, keeping each kind separate. Heat ½ ounce of the butter in a saucepan. Once it foams, add the Chanterelle mushrooms, don't touch them for 30 seconds, then cook, stirring, for 3–4 minutes, until tender. At the end of the cooking time, season to taste and remove to a bowl. Repeat the process with the rest of the mushrooms, cooking each kind separately.

Peel the parsnips, make them into balls, and glaze them with ¾ oz of the butter and the sugar (glazing recipe on page 12).

Cut the potatoes in half, place them in a saucepan, and add water almost to cover and the coarse salt. Bring the water to a boil and cook for 8 minutes. Drain the potatoes and sauté in a frying pan with the remaining ½ ounce of butter for 2 minutes to brown. Season the potatoes, then smoke them, and the chicken if you like, following the method on page 14.

Serve the chicken in a deep plate with the sauce and vegetables.

Spoiler alert

Who hasn't secretly wanted to start the school year at Hogwarts and be sent by the Sorting Hat to Gryffindor House? Or to play a game of Quidditch with the Weasleys and pull up mandrakes in Professor Sprout's greenhouse? This recipe should please more than one Muggle!

HARRY POTTER

Bertie Bott Chocolate Lava Cakes

MAKES 12 CAKES

Preparation time: 20 mins

Cooking time: 10 mins

2 Eggs

2$^1/_4$ oz Superfine sugar

2$^3/_4$ oz Flour

1 t Baking powder

2$^1/_4$ oz Butter

1$^1/_2$ fl oz Milk

1$^3/_4$ oz Semisweet chocolate

Flavorings, spices, fruit, vegetables

Preheat the oven to 350°F. Whisk together the eggs and sugar in a mixing bowl; the mixture should become a little paler.

Sift the flour and baking powder together and incorporate into the mixture, little by little. Melt the butter (a few seconds in a microwave oven is enough) and add it to the mixture.

Next, add the milk and mix together well. Melt the semisweet chocolate in a double boiler or microwave oven, then stir it into the mixture.

Add a touch of originality to your lava cakes, Bertie Bott style. To do this, divide the batter between several bowls and add a different flavor to every bowl: a vegetable (radish, carrot), a fruit (raspberry, blueberry), a flavor (vanilla, mint), a spice (saffron, cinnamon), a candy . . . wherever your imagination takes you.

Half-fill 12 standard size cupcake liners with this mixture. Place the cakes in the oven and bake for 10 minutes.

Spoiler alert

Bertie Bott's Every Flavor Beans™ are the stand-out candies of the Harry Potter universe. The element of surprise is that you don't know what flavor these beans hold in store for you. The approach is the same with these cakes, but perhaps avoiding the notorious bogey flavor.

THE MATRIX
Matrix Burger

MAKES 8 BURGERS

Preparation time: 30 mins

Cooking time: 1 hr 5 mins

For the burger buns:

3¹⁄₂ fl oz Water

2 t Dried yeast

1 oz Superfine sugar

8 fl oz Milk

2 oz Butter

¹⁄₂ oz Cuttlefish ink

2 Eggs

1¹⁄₄ lb Flour

¹⁄₄ oz Salt

Wasabi sesame seeds

For the filling:

3 Green tomatoes

1 Cucumber

4 Lettuce leaves

14 oz Fresh salmon

3¹⁄₂ oz Smoked salmon

1 Shallot

1 drizzle Olive oil

Salt and pepper

For the wasabi sauce:

4 T Sour cream

8 T Strained yogurt

1 Lemon

Wasabi mustard

Make the burger buns: Preheat the oven to 120°F. Heat the water in a glass in a microwave oven for 1 minute, then add the yeast and the sugar. Heat the milk and butter in a saucepan, then add the cuttlefish ink. Let the milk cool to lukewarm and stir in one of the eggs.

Place half the flour in a stand mixer bowl or mixing bowl with the yeast mixture and the milk mixture. Knead in a stand mixer (medium speed) or by hand. Add the rest of the flour, little by little, and the salt, continuing to knead. Work and stretch the dough. Divide the dough into eight balls, place on a baking sheet, and let rise in the oven for 35 minutes. Take the buns out of the oven and raise the temperature to 350°F.

In a bowl, lightly beat the remaining egg to make the glaze. Brush the balls of dough with the beaten egg and scatter with wasabi sesame seeds to your taste. Bake in the oven for 20 minutes.

Prepare the filling: Slice the tomatoes and cucumber into rounds. Wash the lettuce. Chop the fresh and smoked salmon. Peel and finely dice the shallot. Mix together the salmon and shallots, and season to taste. Shape the salmon into eight patties. Heat the olive oil in a frying pan, and cook the patties for 2 minutes on each side.

Make the wasabi sauce: Mix together the sour cream and strained yogurt. Add the juice of the lemon and wasabi mustard according to taste.

Split the burger buns in half, warm them in the oven for 5 minutes, and assemble the burgers by spreading the buns with the wasabi sauce, then topping with a salmon patty and the salad vegetables.

Spoiler alert

What could be better than eating a great burger before taking a trip through the Matrix?
You wouldn't want to meet the Oracle, see the Woman in the Red Dress, and bump into a few Agents
on an empty stomach.

THE MATRIX
The Offer of Morpheus

SERVES 4
Preparation time: 30 mins
Cooking time: 5 mins

For the purée:
2 Bananas

2 Avocados

1½ oz Superfine sugar

2 Limes

For the caramel:
6 oz Whipping cream

5½ oz Superfine sugar

2¾ oz Salted butter

For the decoration:
2¼ oz Semisweet chocolate

4 Red gummy candies

4 Blue gummy candies

Make the purée: Mash the bananas and avocados in a bowl using a fork. Add the 1½ ounces of sugar and the juice of the limes, then mix together well.

Make the caramel: Heat the cream in a small saucepan. Place the sugar in another saucepan and cook it, without stirring, until a caramel forms. Once the caramel is an amber color, add the cream very gradually, in several stages, stirring constantly with a whisk. Next, incorporate the salted butter in small pieces and mix together.

Prepare the decoration: Melt the semisweet chocolate in a double boiler or for a few seconds in a microwave oven.

Place a layer of caramel in the bottom of each of eight verrines, then a layer of the banana-avocado purée, and finally a thin layer of melted semisweet chocolate. Place a red candy on four of the small glass tumblers and a blue candy on the remaining four. Do this before the chocolate sets so the candy sticks to the top of the dessert.

Spoiler alert

Apart from being the captain of the *Nebuchadnezzar*, Morpheus is also the character who believes most in Neo, convinced he is the much-awaited One who has come to liberate humans from the domination of the machines, as prophesied. But first, he offers Neo a choice: take the blue pill to end the story and return to a life of sweet dreams. Or take the red pill to stay in Wonderland and follow the white rabbit down into the abyss.

THE LORD OF THE RINGS

Sam Gamgee Stew with Nasty Fries and Lembas

—

SERVES 4

Preparation time: 30 mins

Cooking time: 45 mins

For the stew:

2 Saddles of rabbit
(about 1 lb 5 oz)

1 Onion

4 Carrots

3¹/₂ oz White mushrooms

1¹/₂ oz Butter

1 t Honey

1 T + 1¹/₂ oz Flour

2 T Veal bouillon powder

18 fl oz Hot water

1 Bouquet garni

Salt and pepper

Make the stew: Bone the saddles of rabbit (you can ask your butcher to do this, it will be less fiddly). Peel the onion and slice very thinly, peel the carrots and slice into rounds, and cut the mushrooms into quarters.

Melt the butter in a large, heavy saucepan until foamy. Add the onion and sauté with a pinch of salt, some pepper, and the honey to caramelize. Brown the saddles over high heat, then add the carrots and mushrooms. Cook for 2–3 minutes, add 1 tablespoon of flour, and cook for 2 minutes.

Dissolve the bouillon powder in a little water in a bowl, then add the 18 fluid ounces of hot water. Add it to the saucepan with the bouquet garni, cover, and cook for 10–15 minutes. Remove the rabbit and vegetables, and heat the sauce over high heat so it reduces and thickens. Return the rabbit and vegetables to the sauce and adjust the seasoning if needed.

Make the fries: Peel the potatoes and roughly cut them into fries. Place them in a saucepan and add cold water to almost cover and the coarse salt. Bring the water to a boil and allow 1 minute, then drain the fries.

For the fries:

6 Potatoes

1 T Coarse salt

Neutral-flavored oil, e.g. corn

For the lembas:

2 Eggs

2 T Honey

2 T Grapeseed oil

2 T Orange blossom water

2¼ oz Ground almonds

1½ oz Flour

1 t Baking powder

1 pinch Salt

1 pinch Ground star anise

Zest of 1 orange

3 T Pumpkin seeds

4 Large fruit tree leaves
(e.g., fig leaves)

Heat enough oil to cover the base of a frying pan and add the fries. Cook them for a few minutes and season. Check whether they're cooked with the tip of a sharp knife—if the blade comes out easily, they are cooked! You can also hay-smoke the chips if you feel the urge (in that case, follow the method on page 14).

Make the lembas: Preheat the oven to 350°F. Whisk together the eggs with the honey. Stir in the grapeseed oil, orange blossom water, ground almonds, flour, baking powder, a pinch of salt, star anise, orange zest, and pumpkin seeds. Pour the batter into 4 cups in a cupcake pan and bake for 10 minutes.

Remove the cakes from the oven and let them cool, then tie a large fruit tree leaf around each. Arrange the rabbit and vegetables attractively on the plates.

Spoiler alert

If there were to be just one book left in the living room library, it would be this one, my precious!
J. R. R. Tolkien's œuvre spans generations, both in his books and on screen. In the second installment of
the film trilogy, Sam makes a stew with the rabbits Gollum catches, the only way to eat them in his opinion.
Gollum wants nothing to do with the "nasty fries" Sam finds so tempting, but it's certainly a change from
lembas—the elven bread they have in their bags.

THE LORD OF THE RINGS
Sauron Tartlets

SERVES 4

Preparation time: 30 mins

Cooking time: 15 mins

Resting time: 8 mins

For the tartlet base:

1 Egg

2¼ oz Superfine sugar

2¼ oz Flour

¾ oz Milk

¾ oz Olive oil

For the filling:

3½ oz Mascarpone cheese

3½ oz Sour cream

½ oz Superfine sugar

1 pinch Saffron

For the eye decoration:

1¾ oz Semisweet chocolate

2 Mandarins

Make the tartlet base: Preheat the oven to 335°F. Whisk together the egg and the sugar in a mixing bowl; the mixture should become a little paler. Add the flour, milk, and olive oil. Mix together. Pour this mixture into a 9½-inch mold or onto a baking sheet lined with with parchment paper, place in the oven and bake for 15 minutes, then let cool.

Make the filling: Beat the marscarpone cheese, sour cream, and the sugar using a hand mixer or whisk, until the mixture holds soft peaks, then add the saffron. Make sure the ingredients and bowl are very cold so that the mixture whips well.

Prepare the decoration: Melt the chocolate in a double boiler or microwave oven. Pour the melted chocolate onto a sheet of parchment paper and let it cool for 3 minutes. Using a sharp knife, cut out slit shapes to form the pupils of the eye and place the sheet in the refrigerator for 5 minutes. Once the chocolate has hardened, detach the chocolate pupil shapes.

Peel the mandarins and remove the membrane with a sharp knife so you only keep the skinless segments.

Cut out small individual circles in the tartlet base using a round cookie cutter. Place some of the cream mixture on the tartlet bases, add the mandarin segments, and top them with a chocolate pupil.

Spoiler alert

To complete their journey through Middle-earth, Frodo and Sam must go to Mordor to destroy the One Ring in the heart of Mount Doom. Just like our two hobbits, we must end the culinary adventure of this meal at Barad-dûr, face to face with Sauron, the Dark Lord.

STAR WARS

Dagobah Swamp with Herb Crust

—

SERVES 4

Preparation time: 35 mins

Cooking time: 1 hr

1 lb 5 oz Pork tenderloin

Olive oil, for drizzling

5½ oz Gruyère cheese

5½ oz Crustless white bread

Chopped herbs (parsley,
tarragon, chervil)

For the sauce:

2 T Chicken bouillon powder

9 oz Peas

6 Mint leaves

For the vegetables:

1 T Chicken bouillon powder

1 Onion, finely diced

Butter, for frying

1 T Honey

5¾ oz Quinoa

2 Zucchini

12 Asparagus spears

3½ oz Hazelnuts, toasted

Salt and pepper

Preheat the oven to 350°F. Roll the pork tenderloin in a sheet of aluminum foil with a drizzle of olive oil and some salt and pepper. Cook in the oven for 20 minutes. Meanwhile, process the gruyère cheese and bread together in a blender or food processor to make crumbs and add a handful of chopped herbs, to taste. Season with salt and pepper to taste.

Remove the pork from the aluminum foil and lay the herbed bread crumbs on top of the meat. Bake under the broil setting of the oven at 400°F for 5 minutes.

Make the sauce: Dissolve the chicken bouillon powder in 18 fluid ounces water in a saucepan and bring to a boil. Add the peas and mint leaves and cook for 5 minutes. Set aside some peas for the garnish and purée the rest of the mixture in a food processor, then pass through a fine metal strainer to make a runny sauce. Adjust the seasoning if needed.

Prepare the vegetables: Dissolve the chicken bouillon powder in 2 pints (4 cups) hot water. Cook the onion in a saucepan with a knob of butter. Add a pinch of salt and the honey. Once the onion has browned, add the quinoa. Cook over medium heat for 20 minutes, adding the chicken broth little by little until it evaporates completely.

Make balls from the unpeeled zucchini using a melon baller and sauté in a knob of butter in a frying pan. Season. Steam the asparagus for 5 minutes and sauté in a knob of butter in a frying pan. Adjust the seasoning if necessary. Roughly crush a few hazelnuts and toast for 2 minutes in a hot frying pan.

Slice two medallions of pork per person and arrange the different elements on serving plates, sprinkling with the toasted hazelnuts.

Spoiler alert

Everyone loves Yoda—it's a given. He is a wise, small green creature, who can leap from place to place in a flash. Set a course for Dagobah and pay him tribute via this dish reminiscent of his swamp-covered planet.

STAR WARS
Skywalker Verrine

—

SERVES 4

Preparation time: 45 mins

Cooking time: 2 hrs

For the meringue:

2¹/₂ oz Egg whites

3 oz Superfine sugar

For the chocolate cream:

9 fl oz Whipping cream

9 oz Mascarpone cheese

1¹/₂ oz Superfine sugar

3¹/₂ oz White chocolate

1 t Vanilla powder

3¹/₂ oz Dried unsweetened shredded coconut

For the lightsabers:

3¹/₂ oz White chocolate

Fat-soluble blue food coloring

Fat-soluble red food coloring

8 Cookie sticks

Make the meringue: Preheat the oven to 175°F. Whip the egg whites in a stand mixer or with a hand mixer, adding half the sugar when the whites start to froth, then the rest when the meringue starts to form. Continue whipping until you have a glossy meringue. Shape into meringues and bake for 2 hours.

Make the chocolate cream: Whip the cream, mascarpone cheese, and sugar until firm peaks form. Make sure that the mixing bowl, cream, and mascarpone are very cold. Melt the white chocolate in a double boiler or microwave oven, then fold it into the cream. Add the vanilla powder and shredded coconut, mixing together gently.

Make the lightsabers: Melt the white chocolate and divide it between two bowls. Mix the blue coloring into one and the red coloring into the other.

Dip the cookie sticks in the two colored chocolates, leaving one end uncoated to form the hilt, and cool in the refrigerator. Crumble cookies and break up the meringue. To serve, place a little of the crumbled cookies in the bottom of a glass, then the cream, and top with some meringue. Finally, dip a chocolate-covered lightsaber in each dish.

Spoiler alert

One of the most memorable battles in the Star Wars saga takes place in *Episode V: The Empire Strikes Back*, more specifically on the ice planet Hoth. Luke uses various tactics to bring down the AT-AT walkers, which are huge Imperial quadripeds. Hop on your snowspeeder to eat this dessert, and don't forget your lightsaber.

... TV SERIES

BREAKING BAD

Los Pollos Hermanos Fried Chicken

SERVES 4

Preparation time: 1 hr

Cooking time: 35 mins

5 T Flour

1 T Chicken seasoning

2 Eggs

7 oz Cornflakes

20 Chicken tenderloins

2 pt/4 cups Oil for deep-frying

For the Mexican salsa:

2 Tomatoes

2 Bell peppers

2 Onions

Olive oil

1 T Honey

1 Garlic clove

1 Bouquet garni

1 pinch Cayenne pepper

For the potatoes:

12 Fingerling potatoes

1 T Coarse salt

1 T Mexican spices

Prepare three shallow containers: In the first, mix together the flour, chicken seasoning, and a pinch of salt and pepper. In the second, beat the eggs. In the third, crush the cornflakes. Dip the tenderloins first in the flour, then in the beaten egg, and then in the crushed cornflakes.

Heat the frying oil in a saucepan or deep fryer to 335°F. Deep fry the tenderloins in the hot oil for 1 minute then remove and drain on paper towels.

Make the Mexican salsa: Remove the skin of the tomatoes and bell peppers using a tomato peeler. Seed them, then roughly chop the tomatoes and slice the peppers into thin strips. Peel the onions and slice them thinly as well. Sauté the onions in a saucepan with some olive oil and a pinch of salt for 2 minutes. Add the honey to caramelize them slightly. Add the bell peppers, tomatoes, the garlic clove with its sprout removed, the bouquet garni, and cayenne pepper to taste. Cook over medium heat for 25 minutes, to evaporate the liquid released from the vegetables. Adjust the seasoning if necessary.

Prepare the potatoes: Cut them in half lengthwise. Place them in a saucepan with water to almost cover and add the coarse salt. Bring to a boil and cook for 7 minutes, then drain the potatoes and set them aside.

Finish cooking the potatoes in a frying pan with a little oil, salt, pepper, and Mexican spices.

Serve on a plate or in paper cones.

Spoiler alert

Yo b*tches! Stop by the most famous restaurant chain in New Mexico before your appointment with Saul Goodman. Make like Gustavo Fring and treat your guests to that classic fast food, fried chicken!

BREAKING BAD

Donuts and Blue Meth, B*tch!

SERVES 4

Preparation time: 30 mins

Cooking time: 20 mins

For the blue meth:

3 1/2 oz Superfine sugar

1 3/4 oz Glucose syrup

1 3/4 oz Water

1 tiny pinch Blue powdered
food coloring

For the express donuts:

3 1/2 fl oz Milk

3/4 oz Butter

1 1/2 oz Superfine sugar

1 t Instant dried yeast

1 Egg

1 t Vanilla extract

1 t Ground cinnamon

9 oz Flour

Oil for deep frying

3 1/2 oz White chocolate

Make the Blue Meth: Heat the sugar, glucose syrup, water, and blue food coloring in a saucepan until they reach 300°F. Check the temperature with a candy thermometer. Pour the mixture onto a baking sheet and let it cool, then break the sheet of sugar into small crystals.

Make the donuts: Warm the milk and butter in a saucepan or microwave oven. Add the sugar and instant yeast, stir with a whisk, and let stand for 5 minutes. Add the egg, vanilla extract, and cinnamon, and stir. Gradually add the flour and knead by hand or in a stand mixer for at least 5 minutes. Add a little extra flour if the dough sticks too much to your fingers.

Heat the frying oil in a saucepan or deep fryer to reach 325°F–335°F. Make donuts by shaping the dough into rings or balls with a hole in the center, then flattening them slightly. Cook the donuts in the oil for 1–2 minutes, turning them over.

Melt the white chocolate in a double boiler or microwave oven. Dip one side of the donuts in the chocolate. Decorate with the crystals of blue meth and let them cool in a refrigerator.

Spoiler alert

Yo! Albuquerque cops can't seem to get enough donuts. Here's the recipe.
Hurry up and get back in the RV, we need you to pack Mr. White's meth, 99.1 percent pure, b*tch!

DEXTER

Dexter Morgan's Brunch

SERVES 4

Preparation time: 30 mins

Cooking time: 1 hr

For the ketchup:

2¼ lb Tomatoes

1 Onion

½ oz Butter

1 T Honey

1 T Tomato paste

1 sprig Thyme

1 Bay leaf

1 Garlic clove

1½ pt/3 cups Wine vinegar

1½ oz Superfine sugar

1 pinch Espelette pepper

Salt and pepper

For the coffee toasts:

9 oz Mascarpone cheese

¾ oz Superfine sugar

1 T Coffee extract

1 T Chicory root extract

4 slices Bread

For the sides:

4 strips Smoked bacon

4 Quail eggs

Oil, for frying

2 Potatoes

10 fl oz Oil for deep frying

2 blood oranges

Salt

Make the ketchup: Cut the tomatoes into quarters and remove the seeds. Peel the onion, slice very thinly, and cook with the butter, a pinch of salt, and the honey in a saucepan for 5 minutes. Add the tomatoes, tomato paste, thyme, bay leaf, garlic clove with the sprout removed, vinegar, sugar, and Espelette pepper. Cook over medium heat for 30–35 minutes to evaporate as much moisture as possible. Remove the thyme, bay leaf, and garlic clove. Purée the remaining mixture and strain through a fine metal strainer to remove the tomato skin and any remaining seeds. Adjust the seasoning.

Make the coffee toasts: Beat the mascarpone cheese with the sugar, coffee extract, and chicory root extract. Toast the bread and spread with the mixture.

Prepare the sides: Preheat the oven to 350°F. Place the strips of bacon between two baking sheets and bake them in the oven for 20 minutes. Once cooled, reduce them to crumbs. Fry the quail eggs in a frying pan with a drizzle of oil for 2 minutes, so the white is cooked and the yolk is still runny. Peel and thinly slice the potatoes. Heat the oil for deep frying to 350°F in a saucepan or deep fryer. Deep fry the slices of potato for 30 seconds, then drain on paper towels and season with salt. Peel the blood oranges with a knife so the skin and membrane is removed and cut out the skinless segments.

Just like Dexter, don't leave anything to chance and arrange all the elements meticulously on a plate.

Spoiler alert

The credits are a mini episode in themselves, with every part of Dexter's morning ritual having a double meaning related to his dark side.

DEXTER

Key Lime Pie

SERVES 6

Preparation time: 45 mins

Cooking time: 25 mins

Resting time: 2 hrs

For the base:

7 oz Gingerbread cookies

2$\frac{1}{2}$ oz Butter

For the filling:

4 Eggs

4 Limes

10$\frac{1}{2}$ oz Sweetened condensed milk

3$\frac{1}{4}$ oz Superfine sugar

Make the base: Preheat the oven to 350°F. Reduce the gingerbread cookies to crumbs in a food processor. Melt the butter, add it to the gingerbread crumbs, and mix together with a metal spoon. Pour the mixture into a 9$\frac{1}{2}$-inch springform pan and press it down well. Place in the oven and bake for 10 minutes. Cool the crust for a few moments.

Make the filling: Separate the eggs. Place the four yolks in one bowl and two of the whites (2$\frac{1}{2}$ ounces) in another. Grate the zest of two of the limes, then juice all four.

Whisk together the yolks with the sweetened condensed milk, lime juice, and lime zest. Pour this mixture over the crust, place in the oven and bake for 15 minutes. Let cool then let the pie rest for at least 2 hours in the refrigerator.

Place the remaining two egg whites in the bowl of a stand mixer and start it on medium speed (or beat using a hand mixer). When the whites start to froth, add half the sugar. Increase the speed gradually. When the mixture turns white, but is still liquid, add the remaining sugar and increase the speed of the mixer again. Let it run for another 5 minutes, until the meringue is firm.

Decorate the pie with the meringue, then scorch it with a small blowtorch or place it under the oven broiler for 1 minute.

Spoiler alert

In season 3, Dexter is given the job of finding the perfect key lime pie and taking it to Camilla. Once you've tried this Florida specialty, you'll agree it's a killer dessert!

GAME OF THRONES

Joffrey Baratheon's Pigeon Pie

SERVES 4

Preparation time: 30 mins

Cooking time: 30 mins

For the pie:

1 Pigeon

1 Shallot

3 1/2 oz Black trumpet mushrooms

1/2 bunch Italian parsley

1/2 oz Butter

1 T Honey

7 oz Veal sausage meat

2 rolls Shortcrust pastry (about 18 oz)

1 Egg

For the salad:

2 T Rice vinegar

Purple food coloring

4 T Olive oil

7 oz Lettuce

Prepare the pie filling: Bone the pigeon (or ask your butcher to do it) and cut the meat into small pieces. Peel and finely dice the shallot, and chop the black trumpet mushrooms and the parsley.

Cook the shallot over medium heat in a frying pan with the butter, a pinch of salt, and the honey for 3 minutes. Add the mushrooms and cook for another 3 minutes.

Mix together the ingredients for the pie filling (the pigeon and sausage meat and the softened shallot, mushrooms, and parsley) in a mixing bowl.

Preheat the oven to 350°F. Cut out a circle of shortcrust pastry from one pastry sheet that's larger than the tart pan for the base, and a smaller one from the other sheet for the top. Lay the larger circle in the tart pan so the pastry comes right over the edges. Add the filling and place the second circle on top and crimp the edges to seal the pie. Make holes in the top of the pie so steam can escape.

Break the egg into a bowl and lightly beat it. Brush the pie with the beaten egg to glaze, then bake it in the oven for 20 minutes. Make a crown from the pastry offcuts, glaze, and bake for 10 minutes.

Make the salad: Mix together the rice vinegar, a little purple food coloring, and the olive oil in a mixing bowl, then season with salt and pepper. Toss the lettuce with the vinaigrette (or place in plastic eye droppers).

Cut the pie into 4 pieces and serve with the salad.

Spoiler alert

It's a day of celebration in King's Landing, the capital of Westeros. Stark, Lannister, Tyrell . . . representatives of all the Great Houses of the kingdom are present for the king's wedding and celebrate it with great fanfare, before the ceremony takes a rather dramatic turn for certain individuals. *Valar Morghulis!*

GAME OF THRONES
Trio of Westeros Desserts

SERVES 4

Preparation time: 1 hr 30 mins

Cooking time: 1 hr

For the
Highgarden Halfmoons:

14 Agen prunes

2 T Raisins

2 Dried figs

4 Walnuts

3 Eggs

3¹⁄₂ oz Superfine sugar

3¹⁄₂ oz Butter

3¹⁄₂ oz Ground almonds

Zest of 1 orange

1 roll Shortcrust pastry
(about 9 oz)

Make the Highgarden Halfmoons: Preheat the oven to 350°F. Chop the dried fruit finely and roughly crush the walnuts.

Make the almond cream: Whisk together two of the eggs and the sugar in a bowl. Melt the butter and add to the mixture with the ground almonds. Mix together well.

Add the dried fruit and walnuts with the orange zest and mix together.

Cut out circles of shortcrust pastry and place 1 tablespoon of the almond cream mixture in the middle. Moisten the edge of the pastry slightly with a finger dipped in cold water and fold the pastry over to make a crescent shape, sealing the edges by pinching them together. Break the remaining egg in a bowl and beat it with a fork. Brush the crescents with the beaten egg to glaze. Place in the oven and bake for 20 minutes.

For the Dorne Wine Cream:

5 1/2 oz Butter

6 Egg yolks

1 bottle Dry white wine

7 oz Superfine sugar

5 1/2 oz Brioche

1 pinch Saffron

For the Hot Pie Cookies:

10 1/2 oz Brioche

4 T Water

4 T Milk

1 3/4 oz Ground almonds

2 t/1/4 oz Baking powder

3 Egg yolks

1 pinch Cinnamon

1 pinch Ground star anise

1 T Honey

Pinch of salt

Make the Dorne Wine Cream: Cut the butter into pieces and leave at room temperature for 30 minutes. Mix the egg yolks into the butter with 4 tablespoons of dry white wine, add the sugar, and whisk together. Blend this butter with the brioche in a food processor.

Boil the rest of the bottle of wine in a saucepan for 10 minutes to evaporate the alcohol. Add the brioche-butter mixture and cook, stirring constantly with a whisk, for 5 minutes, or until the cream thickens slightly. Once it has thickened, stir in the saffron and let cool. Pour the wine cream into verrines.

Make the Hot Pie cookies: Preheat the oven to 350°F. Process all the ingredients together in a food processor. If the dough sticks too much to your fingers, add a little flour so you can work with it more easily. Shape the dough into wolf-shaped cookies and prick them with a fork or knife.

Arrange the cookies on a baking sheet lined with parchment paper and bake for 15–20 minutes, until golden.

Serve these three mini desserts with a hot drink for an indulgent Made-in-Westeros high tea.

Spoiler alert

Sent to the Wall to join the Night's Watch? Before you leave, have a little dessert! The quality of Dorne wine is well known—the sun of Highgarden has once again produced good fruit this year and the young orphan Hot Pie is still making his famous wolf-shaped cookies at the inn. Safe journey and "Now your watch begins . . . "

THE BIG BANG THEORY

Pad Thai between Friends

SERVES 4

Preparation time: 1 hr

Cooking time: 20 mins

9 oz Rice noodles

2 T Tamarind paste

5½ oz Tofu

2 Scallions (or 2 spring onions)

2 Shallots

3½ oz Unsalted peanuts

Sunflower oil

12 Shrimp, peeled

2 T Fish sauce

8 T Demerara sugar

2 Eggs

5½ oz Fresh bean sprouts

1 pinch Espelette pepper
(or mild chili powder)

Juice of 1 Lime

Salt and pepper

Soak the rice noodles in cold water for 15 minutes and drain. Dilute the tamarind paste in a cup of hot water for 10 minutes. Dice the tofu. Thinly slice the scallions and shallots. Roughly chop the peanuts.

Pour 2 tablespoons of sunflower oil into a wok. When the oil is very hot, add the tofu and peeled shrimp, and cook for 1 minute, then set them aside in a bowl.

Add more oil to the wok if needed, and, when it is very hot, add the scallions and shallots and let them cook for 2 minutes. Next, add the tamarind, fish sauce, and demerara sugar. Let this mixture cook and reduce so it caramelizes slightly. Then add the rice noodles and cook for 2 minutes, adding a little water if necessary to finish cooking the noodles.

Meanwhile, beat the eggs and cook them in a frying pan, stirring constantly to make scrambled eggs.

Add the eggs to the mixture in the wok with the bean sprouts, peanuts, tofu, and shrimp. Stir everything together for 1 minute to heat through and combine well.

Adjust the seasoning, and add Espelette pepper and lime juice to taste.

Serve the Pad Thai in a bowl or a cardboard noodle box (oyster pail) for a takeout look.

Spoiler alert

Sheldon and Leonard often have their friends over to share dishes from their favorite Asian takeout restaurant. Now you, too, can be a geek and spend time in the living room discussing politics in Klingon. Bazinga!

THE BIG BANG THEORY

Cheesecake Factory

SERVES 8

Preparation time: 30 mins

Cooking time: 40 mins

Resting time: 4 hrs minimum

For the crust:

7 oz Gingerbread cookies, crushed

2 3/4 oz Butter

For the filling:

2 Eggs

5 3/4 oz Superfine sugar

Juice of 1 lime

1 lb 2 oz Mascarpone cheese

10 1/2 oz Cream cheese

1 T Vanilla extract

Preheat the oven to 350°F.

Make the crust: Place the gingerbread cookies in the bowl of a food processor and reduce them to crumbs. Set aside in a bowl. Melt the butter in a microwave oven, add it to the gingerbread crumbs, and mix together with a metal spoon.

Pour the crumb mixture into a 9 1/2-inch springform pan and press it down well. Place in the oven and bake for 10 minutes. Let it cool for a few moments.

Make the filling: Beat the eggs with the sugar using a whisk until the mixture is a little paler and fluffier. Add the lime juice and mix together. Add the mascarpone cheese, cream cheese, and vanilla extract, and mix again.

Lower the temperature of the oven to 325°F. Pour the filling over the crust, place in the oven, and bake for 30 minutes. When it is ready, the cheesecake should still be a little undercooked and wobbly in the middle—it will firm up as it chills.

Chill the cheesecake for at least 4 hours in the refrigerator before serving.

Spoiler alert

You can't go to Pasadena without visiting Penny in her workplace and succumb to the temptation of the restaurant's specialty, cheesecake.

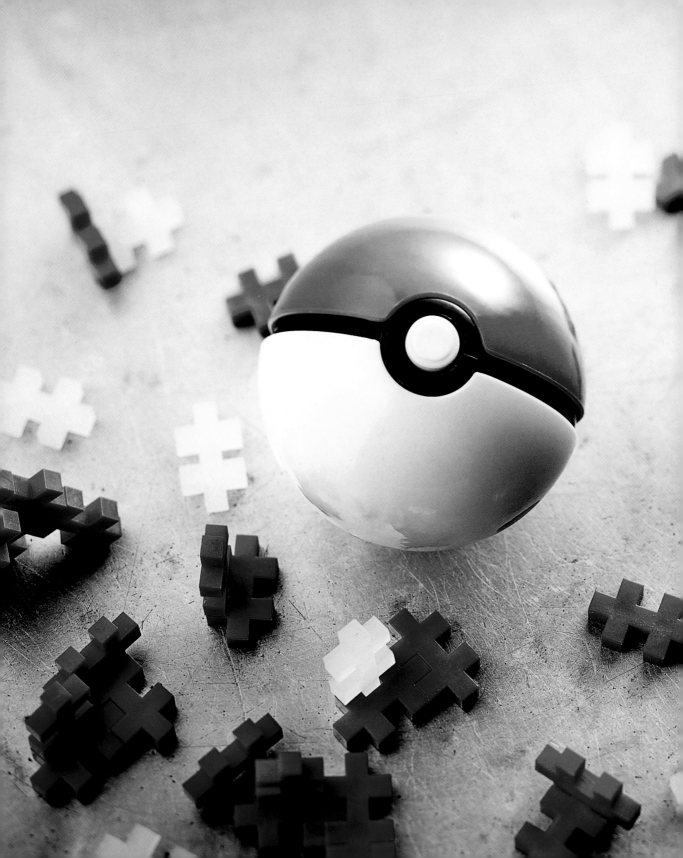

...VIDEO GAMES

MINECRAFT

Cooked Fish with Golden Carrots, Pumpkin, and Beet Sauce

SERVES 4

Preparation time: 40 mins

Cooking time: 45 mins

9 oz Bulgur wheat

For the beet sauce:

7 oz Red beets

1 T Chicken bouillon powder

1 T Mustard

2 T Balsamic vinegar

For the fish:

4 Bream

Olive oil

For the vegetables:

14 oz Pumpkin

4 Yellow carrots

1¼ oz Butter

1 T Superfine sugar

Salt and pepper

Preheat the oven to 350°F.

Bring 2 pints (4 cups) salted water to a boil in a saucepan, add the bulgur wheat, and cook for 10 minutes.

Make the beet sauce: Steam the beets until tender then peel and dice them. Dissolve the chicken bouillon powder in a cup of water. Pour this broth into a saucepan and add the diced red beets. Cook over medium heat for 10 minutes. Add the mustard and balsamic vinegar, purée the sauce with a handheld blender, and adjust the seasoning.

Prepare the fish: Fillet the bream (or ask your fishmonger to do it for you). Remove the bones with tweezers. Heat a drizzle of olive oil in a frying pan and cook the fillets, skin side down, for 1 minute, then season with salt and pepper. Finish cooking in the oven for about 5 minutes. The bream is cooked when bubbles appear on the side of the fillets.

Prepare the vegetables: Chop the pumpkin into small squares. Cook over high heat in a frying pan with 1/2 ounce of the butter and season to taste with salt and pepper.

Glaze the yellow carrots with the remaining butter and the sugar, according to the recipe on page 12.

Place some sauce on each plate, then place the fish on top and the vegetables all around.

Cheat sheet

For this dish, you will obviously need to transform objects using the crafting grid. The items can be easily obtained, but don't forget the gold nuggets and coal. The end result will fully restore your hunger bar and saturation points.

MINECRAFT
Cookies

MAKES 20 COOKIES

Preparation time: 30 mins

Cooking time: 10–15 mins

9 oz Butter

2 Eggs

7 oz Demerara sugar

1 t Baking powder

13 oz Flour

5$^1/_2$ oz Chocolate chips

1$^3/_4$ oz Sesame seeds

Preheat the oven to 400°F.

Melt the butter in a saucepan or microwave oven. Whisk the eggs and sugar together well until they are slightly frothy. Add the melted butter and baking powder, then mix again. Incorporate the flour little by little. Finally, add the chocolate chips and sesame seeds.

Shape the dough into twenty balls. Place the balls on a baking sheet lined with parchment paper and flatten them slightly.

Place in the oven and bake for 10–15 minutes, until golden. Cool and enjoy.

Cheat sheet

You can trade to get cookies, but it is always more worthwhile to craft them from wheat and cocoa beans. While cookies don't do much to restore hunger or saturation, the previous dish is loaded with these points, so there's room for a little sweetness!

ZELDA
Bottle of Elixir Soup

SERVES 4

Preparation time: 30 mins

Cooking time: 30 mins

1 Onion

2 Carrots

1 Yellow bell pepper

14 oz Butternut squash

1 T Chicken bouillon powder

Olive oil

1 T Honey

7 fl oz Whipping cream

Salt and pepper

Peel the onion and carrots. Do the same with the bell pepper and butternut squash, then remove the seeds. Dice all the vegetables, keeping the onion separate.

Dissolve the chicken bouillon powder in a little water in a bowl, then add 2 pints (4 cups) water.

Heat enough oil to cover the base of a saucepan and add the onion with a pinch of salt. Cook for 1 minute, then add the honey. Next, add the carrots, bell pepper, and butternut squash with another pinch of salt. Cook for 5-10 minutes over medium heat, until softened. Add the chicken broth, bring to a gentle simmer, and cook for about 20 minutes. Add the cream and purée the soup using a handheld blender.

If the soup is too thick, add a little water. If it is too thin, cook it a little more to reduce it. Adjust the seasoning and serve.

Cheat sheet

This is Link's favorite soup, which he is given by his grandma after curing her illness. Grandma's soup restores his health and heals his magic. It is stored in a bottle containing two doses, the perfect elixir for searching for fragments of the Triforce.

FINAL FANTASY

Stuffed Cabbage Rolls, Coerthan Carrots, and Sweet Popotoes

SERVES 4

Preparation time: 1 hr 30 mins

Cooking time: 30 mins

8 Cabbage leaves

For the mushroom stuffing :

1 Onion

1 lb 2 oz White mushrooms

1 T Veal bouillon powder

7 oz Thick-cut bacon

For the vegetables:

4 Carrots, glazed (see p. 12)

2 ³/₄ oz Butter

1 T Superfine sugar

1 lb 10 oz Sweet potato

1 T Coarse salt

1 Tonka bean

Salt and pepper

Bring 2 pints (4 cups) salted water to a boil in a saucepan. Submerge the cabbage leaves in the boiling water for 2 minutes, then take them out and plunge them into a large container of cold water. Drain well.

Prepare the stuffing: Peel and finely dice the onion. Wash and slice the mushrooms very thinly, and dissolve the veal bouillon powder in a cup of hot water.

Cut the bacon into lardons and sauté in a dry frying pan. Add the diced onion and cook for 3 minutes. Add the mushrooms and cook for another 3 minutes. Add the cup of veal stock and let it reduce to thicken the sauce.

Lay two cabbage leaves in a greased half-sphere mold or a small bowl, then place some mushroom stuffing inside. Pack down well and fold over the cabbage to enclose the stuffing. Turn over the mold or bowl to unmold the cabbage.

Prepare the vegetables: Glaze the carrots with ³/₄ oz of the butter and the sugar (recipe on page 12). Peel and dice the sweet potatoes. Place in a saucepan, add water almost to cover, add the coarse salt and simmer for 12 minutes. Drain the sweet potatoes, return them to the saucepan with the remaining butter, and mash them to make a purée. Grate the tonka bean over top of the mixture, season with salt and pepper, and mix in.

Place a stuffed cabbage roll on one side of the plate, arrange the carrots, and add dots of sweet potato purée.

Cheat sheet

This dish is the ideal meal to give your character certain attributes (Determination +4%, Vitality +3%, Critical Hit Rate +2%). Serve with Coerthan Carrot and sweet potato to increase them even more.

FINAL FANTASY
Noscean Toast and Spiced Tea

SERVES 4

Preparation time: 30 mins

Cooking time: 20 mins

For the Noscean toast:

2 Eggs

14 fl oz Milk

3 T Maple syrup

1 Vanilla bean

4 slices Slightly stale bread

Olive oil

2 balls Mozzarella cheese (4½ oz each)

8 Walnuts

For the spiced tea:

4 Cardamom pods

¼ oz Ginger root

1 pinch Cinnamon

1 Star anise

2 Cloves

4 Tea bags

1 pinch Espelette pepper

Make the Noscean toast: Lightly beat the eggs in a bowl. Add the milk and maple syrup. Split the vanilla bean in half and scrape out the seeds, then add it to the egg mixture. Mix together.

Soak the slices of bread in this mixture, turning them over so they are well soaked.

Heat a little olive oil in a frying pan. Add the slices of bread and brown them for 4 minutes on each side.

Slice the balls of mozzarella cheese. Roughly crush the walnuts.

Make the spiced tea: Crush the cardamom pods. Peel and chop the ginger root. Heat 2 pints (4 cups) water in a saucepan with the cardamom, ginger, cinnamon, star anise, and cloves, and simmer for 10 minutes. Add the tea bags and let them brew for 3 minutes, then add the Espelette pepper.

Strain the tea to remove the spices and ginger, and serve. Serve the toast by arranging a few slices of mozzarella on the bread and sprinkle with walnuts.

Cheat sheet

To finish your meal and return to the guild, head to Ul'dah for a delicious spiced tea (Piety+4%, Vitality+3%, Speed+2%), or perhaps you'd rather go via the Carline Canopy to enjoy Noscean toast in the company of Miounne (Parry+4%, Vitality+3%, Accuracy+2%)?

... COMICS and
ANIMATION

THE WALKING DEAD

Fresh Flesh Tartare with Soy Mayonnaise

SERVES 4

Preparation time: 1 hr

Cooking time: 10 mins

For the tartare:

1 lb 5 oz Rump steak

1 Shallot

4 Cornichons (baby pickled cucumbers)

1 oz Capers

1 sprig Italian parsley

3 T Sesame oil

8 drops Tabasco sauce

3 T Worcestershire sauce

Espelette pepper
(or mild chili powder)

Salt

For the soy mayonnaise:

3 T Thick soy cream

1 T Mustard

5 fl oz Grapeseed oil

Salt and pepper

On the side:

1 Daikon radish

4 Red radishes

4 Potatoes

1 t Salt

1½ oz Butter

Make the tartare: Using a very sharp knife, finely chop the rump steak into $\frac{1}{8}$–$\frac{1}{4}$ inch dice. Peel and finely dice the shallots. Chop the cornichons, capers, and parsley. Place the prepared ingredients in a bowl, add the sesame oil, Tabasco sauce, Worcestershire sauce, and Espelette pepper, and mix together. Adjust the seasoning to your taste.

Make the soy mayonnaise: Mix together the soy cream and mustard in a bowl. Whisk vigorously and pour in the grapeseed oil little by little, whisking constantly. Season with salt and pepper.

Prepare the vegetables: Peel thin strips of daikon radish to make radish "ribbons." Roll these ribbons into small rings. Slice the red radishes into thin rounds. Peel the potatoes and cut into chunks.

Place the potatoes in a saucepan and add water to almost cover and the salt. Bring to a boil and cook for 10 minutes.

Smoke the potatoes over hay, following the recipe on page 14. Return the potatoes to the saucepan over medium heat, mash them with a fork (leaving some lumps), add the butter, and adjust the seasoning.

Make an attractive arrangement on a plate with the tartare, a few dots of mayonnaise, and the vegetables.

Comic note

Turning rotting flesh into a gastronomic dish is quite a challenge. Take a comic book, zombies, a dash of crazy, and mix it all together. In the fight to keep his group of survivors alive, Rick would do well to sit down for a few minutes and eat a nice tartare before returning to the search for the perfect refuge.

THE WALKING DEAD

Rose-Lychee Jellied Eye with Zombie Fingers and Bloody Coulis

SERVES 4

Preparation time: 1 hr

Cooking time: 1 hr

For the jellied eye:

4 sheets Gelatin

5 fl oz Water

3 T Rose water

Pink food coloring

1 T Superfine sugar

4 Black grapes

4 Lychees

Oil

For the zombie fingers:

2 Apples

1 rectangular sheet Puff pastry

3 T Demerara sugar

12 Whole blanched almonds

1 Egg

For the bloody coulis:

2 3/4 oz Raspberries

2 3/4 oz Redcurrants

7 fl oz Organic beet juice

1 oz Superfine sugar

Make the jellied eye: Soak the sheets of gelatin in a bowl of cold water for 15 minutes. Heat the 5 fl oz water, rose water, one drop of pink food coloring, and sugar in a saucepan. As soon as it comes to a boil, turn off the heat, squeeze out the sheets of gelatin and add them to the liquid. Stir to dissolve the gelatin. Place one grape inside each lychee.

Oil some half-sphere molds so you can easily unmold the jellied eyes. Pour the rose water mixture into these molds, plus a grape-filled lychee. Place the molds in the refrigerator to set the gelatin.

Make the zombie fingers: Preheat the oven to 335°F. Peel and slice the apples very thinly. Place them in a glass bowl and bake in a microwave oven for 1 minute to soften. Cut the puff pastry into 12 rectangles.

Place some cooked apple slices on each rectangle, sprinkle with demerara sugar and roll up the rectangles to make fingers. Place a blanched almond on the end of each pastry finger to make fingernails. Lightly score the dough with a knife to mark the knuckles. Beat the egg in a bowl and brush the pastry fingers to glaze them. Place in the oven and bake for 20–25 minutes, until the pastry is well risen and golden.

Make the bloody coulis: Wash the berries and remove the redcurrants from their stems. Cook the beet juice, berries, and sugar for 10 minutes over medium heat in a saucepan. Blend the mixture in a food processor and strain through a fine metal strainer to remove the seeds.

Splash 1 spoonful of coulis on the plate to look like blood spatter. Finish by adding three zombie fingers and a jellied eye.

Comic note

It's not easy living with zombies, especially when all they think about is eating you.
So naturally, when clean and tidy human beings meet a horde of disgusting undead, there will be blood!

POKÉMON
Meringue Poké Balls

SERVES 4

Preparation time: 1 hr

Cooking time: 2 hrs

For the meringue:

2 ¹/₂ oz Egg whites

3 oz Superfine sugar

1 dash Red powdered food coloring

For the filling:

9 oz Mascarpone cheese

9 fl oz Whipping cream

1 ¹/₂ oz Superfine sugar

3 ¹/₂ oz Caramel-flavored milk chocolate

3 ¹/₂ oz Peanuts

4 Gummy bears

For the decoration:

3 ¹/₂ oz Black fondant icing

Make the meringue: Preheat the oven to 175°F. Whip the egg whites in a stand mixer or with a hand mixer, add half the sugar when the whites start to froth, then add the remaining sugar when the whites start to hold their shape. Continue whipping until they form a glossy meringue. Place half of the meringue in a bowl, add the red food coloring, and mix. Use the leftover plain meringue for the other halves of the Poké Balls.

Line 4 half-sphere molds with the red meringue mixture, leaving enough of a hollow in the middle to fill later on. Bake them for at least 2 hours at 175°F. Repeat this step with the white meringue. Cook and unroll the halves delicately.

Make the filling: Whip the mascarpone cheese, cream, and sugar in a bowl until firm peaks form. Make sure that the mixer bowl, cream, and mascarpone are very cold so that the cream whips well.

Melt the chocolate in a microwave oven or double boiler. Add 2–3 tablespoons of the whipped cream and mix in. Pour this mixture into the rest of the whipping cream and stir again.

Roughly crush the peanuts. Place a Pokémon (gummy bear) inside each meringue hemisphere, fill with the chocolate cream, and sprinkle with peanuts to create a solid crunchy base for the meringue hemisphere.

Make thin strips from the black fondant. Finish the Poké Balls by connecting the red and white halves with the black fondant strips.

Comic note

Collecting Pokémon is fun, but you need to know where to keep them.
Trainers have three options: rent a zoo, buy a customized litter box for each one, or get a supply of Poké Balls. It's not a difficult choice, is it?

BATMAN
Harvey Dent

SERVES 4

Preparation time: 45 mins

Cooking time: 1 hr 45 mins

1 T Chicken bouillon powder

4 Chicken breast fillets

For the cola sauce:

1½ pt/3 cups Cola

1 T Balsamic vinegar

¼ Licorice roll

2 T Veal bouillon powder

For the rice:

4½ oz Basmati rice

4½ oz Black rice

For the garnish:

4 Turnips

¾ oz Butter

1 T Superfine sugar

Black radish

Coarse salt

1 oz Popcorn kernels

Olive oil

1 oz Goji berries

Salt and pepper

Heat 2 pints (4 cups) of water in a saucepan with the chicken bouillon powder. Add the chicken fillets and cook on a very gentle simmer for 15 minutes.

Make the cola sauce: Pour the cola into a saucepan and cook until it reduces to a caramel. There should be the equivalent of 1–2 tablespoons liquid left. Add the balsamic vinegar and licorice. Dissolve the veal bouillon powder with a little water, then add a cup of water. Add this to the cola caramel and cook for 10 minutes over medium heat.

Prepare the rice: Bring 2 pints (4 cups) salted water to a boil in a saucepan, add the basmati rice, and cook for 10 minutes. Rinse the black rice and put it in a saucepan with 2 pints (4 cups) of cold salted water. Bring the water to a boil and cook for 35 minutes.

Prepare the garnish: Glaze the turnips with the butter and sugar, according to the recipe on page 12.

Cut thin slices of black radish, place them in a bowl with some coarse salt for 20 minutes to draw out their liquid, then rinse and pat dry. Make a cut from the middle to the edge and shape the slice into a cone.

Cook the corn kernels for 5 minutes in a saucepan with a little olive oil to make popcorn. Season with salt once popped.

Arrange the two rices in the middle of the plate using a cookie cutter so you have two sides: one black and one white. Place the chicken on the rice. Place the glossy turnip balls and radish cones on one side of the plate, and place the popcorn, sauce, and goji berries on the other side.

Comic note

White or black rice? Turnip or radish? Like Two-Face, let fate decide by flipping a coin. Alternatively, you could make both to conjure resemblance to a memorable villain from this American blockbuster with a totally deconstructed dish.

BATMAN

The Joker

SERVES 4

Preparation time: 1 hr
Cooking time: 20 mins
Resting time: 50 mins

For the berry coulis:

3½ oz Strawberries
3½ oz Raspberries
7 fl oz Cranberry juice
1 T Sugar (optional)

For the violet gelatin:

4 sheets Gelatin
7 fl oz Water
1 dash Violet syrup
1 drop Purple food coloring

For the pistachio cream:

9 oz Mascarpone cheese
2 T Pistachio paste

For the crumble:

¾ oz Superfine sugar
1 oz Ground almonds
¾ oz Flour
1 oz Butter
1 oz Pistachios
1 oz Pumpkin seeds

For the mini candy apples:

1 Granny Smith apple
3½ oz White chocolate

Make the berry coulis: Wash the strawberries and raspberries and cook them in the cranberry juice for 10 minutes in a saucepan, adding 1 tablespoon of sugar if the fruit is too acidic, then blend in a food processor.

Make the violet gelatin: Soak the sheets of gelatin in a bowl of cold water for 15 minutes. Heat the 7 fl oz water with the violet syrup and purple food coloring. Add the softened gelatin sheets and mix in. Pour into rectangular molds and refrigerate for 25 minutes to set the gelatin.

Make the pistachio cream: Beat together the mascarpone cheese and pistachio paste with a whisk to make a firm cream. Place in a pastry bag and set aside in the refrigerator.

Make the crumble: Preheat the oven to 350°F. Mix together the sugar, ground almonds, flour, and butter. Let this mixture rest in the refrigerator for 15 minutes, then break into pieces. Place in the oven and bake for 10 minutes. Crush the pistachios and pumpkin seeds and mix them with the crumble.

Make the mini candy apples: Make balls of apple using a melon baller and insert a stick in each. Meanwhile, melt the white chocolate and mix in the purple fat-soluble food coloring. Dip the apple balls in the colored chocolate and place the mini candy apples in the refrigerator for 10 minutes to set the chocolate.

Pipe the pistachio cream on the violet gelatin in the middle of the plate and scatter with the crumble. Place a mini candy apple alongside and streak some berry coulis on the edge of the plate to make the Joker's "smile."

Comic note

Of all the scarred villains, the Joker has to be the creepiest. Charismatic, completely insane, and the king of the punchline, he has all the qualities to make him Batman's greatest adversary.

TV Dinners for Geeky Evenings

Here are some suggestions for your game evenings with friends . . .

Shrimp Tempura

SERVES 4. Preparation time: 10 mins • Cooking time: 1 min

1 Egg • 5 fl oz Iced water • 3¹/₂ oz Flour • Salt • 1 Ice cube • 12 Large shrimp • 10 fl oz Oil for deep frying

Beat the egg and iced water together in a bowl using a whisk. Add the flour little by little and some salt, then add the ice cube.

Peel the shrimp.

Heat the oil in a saucepan or deep fryer to about 350°F. Dip the shrimp in the batter to coat, then deep fry in the oil for about 1 minute, until golden brown.

Vegetable Dips

SERVES 4. Preparation time: 15 mins

2 Carrots • 8 Radishes • ¹/₂ Cucumber

For the first dip • *2 T Ketchup • 2 T Mayonnaise • Tabasco sauce • 1 T Whiskey (optional)*
For the second dip • *4 Chives • 1 Lemon • 4 T Sour cream • Salt and pepper*

Peel the vegetables, then cut them into sticks using a very sharp knife.

Make the first dip: In a bowl, mix together the ketchup, mayonnaise, a few drops of Tabasco sauce, and the whiskey (if using).

Make the second dip: Snip the chives. Juice the lemon. Mix together the sour cream, lemon juice, and chives. Season to taste with salt and pepper.

Olive Tapenade

SERVES 4. Preparation time: 10 mins

¹/₂ Garlic clove • 7 oz Black pitted olives • 1 T Capers • 6 Anchovy fillets
3 T Olive oil • 12 Breadsticks

Chop the garlic.

Place the garlic, olives, capers, anchovies, and olive oil in the bowl of a food processor.

Process until smooth.

Serve with breadsticks.

Mini-Gyro

SERVES 4. Preparation time: 15 mins • Cooking time: 5 mins
2 Pita breads • 8 Chicken tenderloins • 1 T Olive oil • Spices (paprika, cumin, ground coriander)
3 Lettuce leaves • 1 Tomato • 1 Red onion • Pita sauce

Cook the pita breads in a microwave oven for 30 seconds to puff them up. Cut them into four pieces.

Cook the chicken tenderloins in a frying pan for 5 minutes with the olive oil. Sprinkle generously with paprika, cumin, and ground coriander (about 1 teaspoon of each).

Shred the lettuce leaves. Slice the tomato into rounds. Peel the red onion and slice it into rings.

Place inside each bread pocket some pita sauce, 1 tenderloin, a little lettuce, 1 slice of tomato, and 1 onion ring.

Cheese Twists

SERVES 4. Preparation time: 10 mins • Cooking time: 10 mins
1 roll Puff pastry (about 9 oz) • 3 1/2 oz Shredded cheddar cheese • Pepper

Preheat the oven to 350°F. Cut thin strips of puff pastry (about 1/2 inch) using a knife.

Lay the strips of pastry on a baking sheet lined with parchment paper. Turn the pastry strips to make twists.

Sprinkle with shredded cheddar and pepper.

Cook in the oven for 10 minutes.

Fruit Salad with Espelette Pepper

SERVES 4. Preparation time: 10 mins
1 Mango • 8 Lychees • 3 1/2 oz Raspberries • 7 fl oz Orange juice • 1 1/2 fl oz Lychee liqueur (optional)
• 3 pinches Espelette pepper (or mild chili powder)

Peel and dice the mango. Cut the lychees in four. Wash the raspberries.

Mix together the fruits, orange juice, and lychee liqueur (if using) in a bowl and season with Espelette pepper according to taste.

Serve in verrines.

Useful Measurements

1 SMALL KNOB BUTTER =
1/8 ounce

1 KNOB BUTTER = 1/2 ounce

1 TEASPOON =
→ **1/8** ounce salt, sugar, or oil
→ **1/4** ounce butter
→ **1/8** fluid ounce liquid
→ **1/8** ounce flour or semolina

1 TABLESPOON =
→ **1/2** ounce sugar, flour, or butter
→ **1/3** ounce crème fraîche or oil
→ **1/2** fluid ounce liquid
→ **3** teaspoons

1 PINCH SALT =
0.3-0.5 gram

1 SUGAR CUBE =
1/8 ounce

Oven Temperatures

THERMOSTAT	TEMPÉRATURE APPROXIMATIVE
1	**86°F** (slightly lukewarm)
2	**140°F** (warm)
3	**194°F** (very mild heat)
4	**248°F** (mild heat)
5	**302°F** (moderate heat)
6	**356°F** (medium heat)
7	**410°F** (slightly hot)
8	**464°F** (hot)
9	**518°F** (very hot)
10	**572°F** (extremely hot)

Index

www.facebook.com/chefLigo and www.facebook.com/cuisinepourlesgeeks